WHAT'S IT LIKE TO BE A...?

FORENSIC SCIENTIST

Elizabeth Dowen   Lisa Thompson

First published in the UK 2009 by
A & C Black Publishing Ltd
36 Soho Square
London
W1D 3QY
www.acblack.com

Copyright © 2009 Blake Publishing
Published 2008 by Blake Education Pty Ltd, Australia

ISBN: 978-1-4081-1427-8

A CIP catalogue record for this book is available from the British Library.

Written by Lisa Thompson and Elizabeth Dowen
Publisher: Katy Pike
Editor: Emma Waterhouse
Cover Design: Terry Woodley
Designer: Rob Mancini and Clifford Hayes
Printed in Singapore by Tien Wah Press.

Cover image © Jim Varney/Science Photo Library

All inside images © Shutterstock except p34 (bl) (aap)

This book is produced using paper made from wood grown in managed,
sustainable forests. It is natural, renewable and recyclable. The logging and
manufacturing processes conform to the environmental regulations of the
country of origin.

All the Internet addresses given in this book were correct at the time of
going to press. The author and publishers regret any inconvenience caused
if addresses have changed or sites have ceased to exist, but can accept no
responsibility for any such changes.

Contents

EViDENCE – tHE tRUE WitNESS

Logging onto my computer first thing – what awaits me today?

It's 8:30 am, and I have just arrived at the crime lab.

I get a call from Chris Howard, a crime-scene investigator for the lab. He tells me he has just finished collecting evidence from a crime scene – a home invasion and robbery, where a victim was assaulted and robbed. The perpetrators fled the scene in a stolen car.

The victim is on the way to hospital in a critical condition. Police are still interviewing witnesses and neighbours. They have some leads, but need the help of my team to analyse evidence. The perpetrators are still at large, so answers are needed quickly.

I tell Chris that my team and I will be ready to analyse the evidence as soon as he gets it to the lab.

Hi Alex, the crime-scene evidence is on its way.

What is forensic science?

The term *forensic* technically relates to anything associated with a court of law, public discussion or debate. We more generally know it as the process of gathering evidence to solve a crime. Forensic science is different from other sciences in that it is the examination of material, specifically for use in court.

Forensic science uses many scientific disciplines. Chemical tests, identification of hair, blood, dirt and cloth fibres, DNA testing, microscopy, forensic psychology and forensic medicine are just a few of the many science strands used in the analysis of evidence.

examining
trace
evidence

Where did it come from?

The word *forensic* originated from the 17th century Latin word *forensis*, meaning forum, a place for discussion. Forensic specifically refers to something relating to, connected with or used in a court of law.

A forensic scientist may specialise in the following fields:

Forensic anthropology – the identification of skeletal human remains

Forensic entomology – the examination of insects on and around human remains, to assist in identifying the time and location of death

forensic geology

Forensic biology – DNA analysis of fluids to identify an individual

Forensic odontology – the study of teeth

Forensic toxicology – the study of the effect of drugs and poisons on and in the human body

Forensic geology – the study of trace evidence such as soils, minerals and petroleum

Forensic psychology – the study of a person's mind, usually to determine reasons behind a criminal's behaviour.

The work of a forensic scientist can be divided into three areas:

1 **Field work – collecting the evidence**
   Field work is investigating a crime scene, for example fire and explosion scenes.

2 **Laboratory work – analysing the evidence**
   This includes medical expertise and laboratory work.

3 **Court work – presenting the evidence**
   This includes testifying in court, preparing documents for court and preparing documents for other scientists, or for presentations.

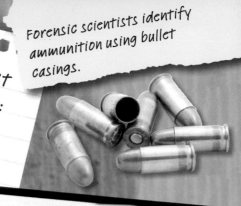

Forensic scientists identify ammunition using bullet casings.

A forensic scientist may perform the following tasks –

- identify illicit drugs
- analyse drugs and poisons in human tissue and body fluids, including blood alcohol levels
- examine and compare materials such as fibres, paints, cosmetics, oils, petrol, plastics, glass, metals, soils and gunshot residues
- DNA profiling
- conduct botanical identification
- conduct document examinations
- examine crime scenes
- identify firearms and ammunition
- detect and identify fingerprints, footprints and tool marks
- analyse tyre marks and tracks
- examine fire and explosion scenes for the origin and cause
- prepare evidence reports for court
- advise police investigators, scientists and pathologists.

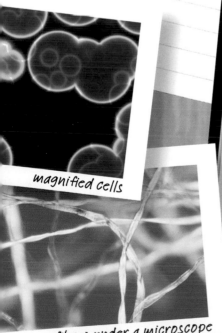

magnified cells

fibres under a microscope

Why I became a forensic scientist

My insect collection was quite impressive!

When I was at school, I developed a passion for science, especially chemistry and biology. I really enjoyed the process of finding answers and solving problems in the science laboratory.

After I left school, I went to university to study biology and chemistry. The laboratory work involved in the course made science all the more exciting and interesting.

People always ask me if it is hard to remain objective, especially if I am working on a high-profile case. I don't think it's hard because forensic science is about the scientific analysis of evidence. It is not about who is involved in the case. Evidence has a way of surprising you – when analysed correctly it cannot lie.

I love putting the pieces of evidence together to help solve a case. With advances in forensic science, like DNA profiling, we are getting faster and better at understanding the evidence we find. All of this keeps the job exciting for me!

The world under a magnifying glass – what a fascinating place!

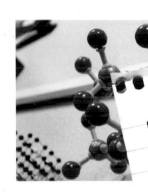

Traits needed for forensic science

- good communication skills
- ability to remain unbiased in the examination of evidence
- meticulous attention to detail
- skilled at clear, logical thinking
- ability to work as part of a team
- motivation to use own initiative
- perseverance
- good observation skills

Forensic science through history

In Roman times, a criminal charge meant presenting the case before a group of people. The person accused of the crime, and the accuser, would both give speeches based on their side of the story. The person with the best argument and delivery would determine the outcome of the case.

Chinese forensics

The book *Xi Yuan Ji Lu* (Collected Cases of Injustice Rectified) written by Chinese author, Song Ci, in 1248, contains one of the earliest written accounts of using medicine and entomology (the study of insects) to solve criminal cases. A death investigator solved one case of a person murdered with a sickle, by asking everyone to bring their sickles to one location. Flies, attracted by the smell of blood, eventually gathered on one sickle. From this evidence, the murderer confessed.

19th century blood tests

In 1875, scientists could not effectively examine dried blood under a microscope. They could not identify blood types, or distinguish between human blood and animal blood.

Fingerprint designs

In 1892, Sir Francis Galton wrote *Fingerprints*, a book about how prints could help solve crimes. Sir Francis worked out the first system for classifying fingerprints. The Galton-Henry system was officially introduced at Scotland Yard in 1901 and quickly became the basis for identification records. His book changed forensic science forever.

DID YOU KNOW?

First glimpse
Anton van Leeuwenhoek (1632–1723), was a Dutch scientist, who was famous for building the first microscope through which it was possible to see single-celled organisms, around 1670.

Edmond Locard (1877-1966)

Edmond Locard was a pioneer in forensic science and became known as the Sherlock Holmes of France. He was an assistant to Alexandre Lacassagne, a professor of Forensic Medicine at the University of Lyon. Locard formulated the basic principle of forensic science – every contact leaves a trace. This is known as Locard's exchange principle.

In 1910, Locard started his own criminal laboratory. He produced a monumental seven-volume work, *Traite de Criminalistique*. In 1918, he developed 12 matching points for fingerprint identification. He continued his research until his death in 1966.

UK burglar caught!

In 1902, Henry (Harry) Jackson was the first person in the United Kingdom convicted on fingerprint evidence. He was a burglar who placed his hands in wet paint during a robbery, thus leaving behind his fingerprints. Can you guess his crime? Jackson stole billiard balls!

Who inspired Sherlock Holmes?

Sherlock Holmes is the fictional character Sir Arthur Conan Doyle created in works he wrote from 1887 to 1915. Conan Doyle based the character of Sherlock Holmes on his teacher, the gifted surgeon and forensic detective Joseph Bell.

Joseph Bell was renowned for being observant. He emphasised the importance of close observation when making a diagnosis. He was even able to deduce the occupation and recent activities of a stranger on the street, simply by observing him.

illustrations from The Adventures of Sherlock Holmes, 1892–1893

The crime scene

Every crime scene is unique. It is important that police seal off the area as quickly as possible, to preserve any potential evidence. The Scenes of Crime Officers (SOCOs) arrive soon after the police, to process the crime scene. People sometimes contaminate evidence by touching things and walking around. Evidence can also disappear shortly after a crime, due to weather or environmental changes.

Civilians are employed by police forces to provide technical services like photography, the collection and comparison of fingerprints, vehicle examination and the detailed examination of scenes of crime.

POLICE DO NOT CROSS

The evidence is recorded.

Crime fighting on TV

Television and movies tend to focus on murder cases, but in reality only a very small proportion of a typical forensic laboratory workload involves homicides. Drugs, robbery, drink driving and fraud are more common areas of investigation.

Documenting crime

The main ways to document crime scenes are through clearly-written notes, sketches, photographs and by recording evidence on video.

Crime-scene notes should include the following information:

- date and time the police were called
- address of the crime and a description of the area
- name of the person who called the crime-scene investigator to the area
- names of the persons who conducted the crime-scene search, including those who took photographs and fingerprints
- weather and lighting conditions
- descriptions and locations of any bodies found
- locations of all evidence found
- descriptions of the interior and exterior of the crime scene
- date and time the crime-scene investigation concluded.

Investigators must have as little physical contact as possible with evidence as they tag, bag and record it. It is vital to leave any material that is collected in its original state.

Crime-scene investigators get to work.

EVIDENCE

The study of physical evidence is the basis of forensic science. Trace evidence is material found at a crime or accident scene in small but measurable amounts. The study of trace evidence relies on Locard's exchange principle, that every contact, no matter how slight, will leave a trace.

Principles behind the gathering of trace evidence

1 Every contact between two people, or between a person and an object or place, leaves evidence on both.

2 Trace evidence that is found, documented and examined, can link a person to a specific time and/or place.

3 Individual characteristics, physical matches and mathematical probability all help identify trace evidence.

Hairy facts

Trichology is the study of hair. The average person has 100,000 hairs on his/her head, with each hair growing about 12.7 cm every year.

Broken glass
Glass is often broken during a crime, and tiny fragments are commonly caught in clothing. They can remain hidden even if the criminal washes the clothes many times over! If the fragments are recovered from the clothing, forensic scientists can analyse them to work out whether they match the glass broken at the crime scene.

Physical evidence is any and every object that:

• establishes a crime has been committed
• provides a link between a crime and its victim
• provides a link between a crime and its perpetrator.

Examples of different kinds of physical evidence
✓ blood and saliva
✓ documents
✓ drugs
✓ explosives
✓ fingerprints
✓ glass
✓ hairs and fibres
✓ insects
✓ firearms, ammunition and gunshot residue
✓ tool marks and impressions
✓ soils and materials
✓ paint chips
✓ tracks or markings

At first glance, wet red soil could be mistaken for blood.

What does the test reveal?

Hair fibres may link a suspect to a crime.

17

A CHAIN OF CUSTODY

After collecting the evidence, it is crucial that the material remains in its original state. To preserve evidence, investigators follow certain procedures to maintain a chain of custody. The name of the collecting official and their signature are recorded, as well as the date and time the evidence was collected, and the location of where it was found.

When sealing the evidence, special tamper-evident seals are used – it is easily seen if they are altered. Recording who had possession of an exhibit and appropriate sealing are critical to proving the reliability of evidence.

collecting evidence

tests conducted back at the lab

IN THE PICTURE

Forensic photography is one part of the evidence-collecting process. Photos are also useful in court as they can visually depict important aspects of the crime scene.

Forensic photography involves choosing correct lighting so images are as clear and accurate as possible. The accurate angling of lenses and a collection of different viewpoints are also important. Pictures often include scales to accurately record the dimensions.

Forensic photography – got to get that angle right!

The Instant Scene Modeller recreates the crime scene.

3D Crime fighting

A company in Toronto, Canada called MDRobotics, has developed the Instant Scene Modeller – a video camera that can record crime scenes. From the data recorded, a computer generates a 3D construction so that investigators can measure items from the crime scene, and play out scenarios, without tampering with evidence. The Instant Scene Modeller can also visually recreate crime scenes for juries and lawyers in a courtroom.

Fingerprints

checking out the prints

Fingerprint analysis is probably the most well-known use of forensic science. In the past, police would spend hours trying to manually match fingerprints to a set in their records. Today, computers can compare one set of fingerprints against half a million others in less than a second. Once the computer identifies potential matches, two forensic scientists then compare the prints separately.

Each fingertip has a pattern of fine skin ridges that are slightly different for each person, even identical twins. Whenever you touch something, you leave behind a faint smear of grease, dust or sweat. The unique pattern on your fingers stays on everything you touch.

Evidence is everywhere – if you look closely enough!

Dacty-what?

Dactyloscopy is the study of fingerprints. It comes from the Greek words *daktylos* meaning finger, and *skopein* meaning to examine.

There are four main patterns for fingerprints:

❶ Arches – formed by ridges running across the finger. About 5 per cent of people have this print.

❷ Whorls – 30 per cent of fingerprints form a complete oval, often in a spiral pattern.

❸ Loops – these have a stronger curve than arches. About 60 per cent of fingerprints have loops.

❹ This group is a mixture of all the patterns.

Which of these is most similar to yours?

DNA on fingerprints!

In the past, DNA analysis was restricted to samples of blood, tissue or bodily fluids such as saliva. Then, in 1996, an Australian team of scientists was the first to prove that DNA can even be analysed from the few skin cells left behind on fingerprints.

I wonder what prints he'll leave behind.

DIDYOUKNOW?

Baby prints
A human foetus acquires fingerprints at three month's gestation.

Lifting a fingerprint

The most common technique for lifting fingerprints is dusting a surface with a very fine powder and a brush. The powder adheres to the oils deposited by fingertips and outlines the ridge details of the prints. The powder prints are then placed onto tape, which is attached to a card, and then sealed in an evidence bag.

Different light wavelengths, or a wide range of chemical treatments, can also detect prints.

Laser scanning

Today, a laser scanning procedure can record new fingerprints by placing the hand on a flat, glass plate. The print is then stored and compared to other prints electronically.

hand scanner

fingerprint powder and brush

Fallible fingerprints

Fingerprint evidence is not infallible. It is subjective and depends on the expert. There have been several cases throughout history and across the globe where convictions were made purely on the basis of fingerprint evidence – but the expert turned out to be wrong.

Sniffing out evidence— Sniffer Dogs

Some evidence at a crime scene is invisible, for example, the scent left behind by people, drugs or explosive products. With their excellent sense of smell, specially-trained dogs can sniff out even the smallest traces of scent. They can also detect human remains and tell the difference between new and older scents.

in training

Me? A sniffer dog?

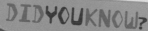
Have I got potential?

DIDYOUKNOW?

Strange things that sniff
Crime-scene investigators may also use a machine that sucks up smells on a scent pad. These scents from the crime scene can be freeze dried and given to a sniffer dog later, to match the scent to a suspect or other evidence.

Bloodstains

Blood, and other body fluids found at a crime scene, may contain crucial physical evidence.

microscope slides

* A bloodstain on either an object or at a location, may prove the use of a weapon, or that a crime has taken place.
* Shape, position, size, or intensity of a bloodstain may support a particular theory of how and when certain events occurred.
* Analysis of DNA from the blood, can eliminate groups of people as suspects.

Blood types

In 1901, scientists found that there are four main human blood groups. These are A, B, AB and O. Types A and O are the most common groups, and type AB is the rarest. Within these types, a person can be Rhesus Factor positive or Rhesus Factor negative. The Rhesus Factor type is written after the ABO type, e.g. A+, O–. Since 1950, scientists have also been able to determine whether blood came from a male or female.

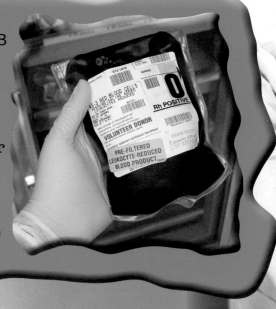

Blood-pattern analysis

Blood-pattern analysis is the study of blood patterns. The type of blood pattern can reveal many things about a crime – where the crime occurred, the number of attackers and the weapons used.

Pools of blood, or smears around a body, show whether it has been dragged. The angle that blood hits a surface, can reveal the direction of the attack. The distance between blood drops, and how far they have splattered, can sometimes indicate where an attack took place and the sequence of an attack.

blood-splatter patterns – droplets, a pool, or a splatter

DID YOU KNOW?

Budding crime-scene investigators take note: a common household bleach can render the forensic techniques for detecting blood useless.

Blood clues

It is very important that investigators consider the surface that bloodstains hit, as well as their size and shape. Where blood hits is very important, because different surfaces will cause different splatter patterns. The harder and less porous the surface, the less the blood will splatter. After a blood drop hits a surface, its shape will either be round or elliptical (oval), which helps determine the direction from which it came.

The harder the surface, the less the blood will splatter.

drops of blood are ball shaped

A drop of blood

A drop of blood is normally spheroid or ball shaped, not the common teardrop shape often depicted. A typical blood drop is around 0.05 ml, and has a falling speed of 6.6 metres per second.

3 parts to blood

There are three main components to blood – red blood cells, platelets and plasma. Red blood cells last for 42 days after collection, platelets last for five days, and plasma, when frozen, lasts for up to one year.

The Luminol test

It is very important to locate weak and invisible stains, any of which may contain valuable evidence. Although the Luminol test cannot conclusively prove stains are blood, it can illuminate invisible stains with a blue light. This test is sensitive enough to pick up minute traces, even when someone has tried to wash them away.

Clotting

The time that blood takes to clot and dry can often indicate when an offence was committed. Blood, after leaving the body, usually takes between three and six minutes to clot.

DNA analysis

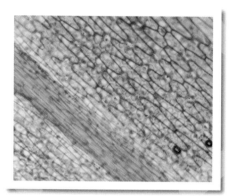

skin cells under a microscope

DNA is a chemical containing all the instructions for making the structures the body needs to function. Every one of our cells has DNA, except red blood cells. Every person is unique – no two people have the same DNA unless they are identical twins.

DNA profiling, or typing, helps police to identify an individual. The process of DNA profiling involves comparing different DNA samples to determine whether or not they could be from the same person.

DNA can be extracted from any body fluid, for example blood, saliva and sweat, or from fragments of a body, like hair roots and skin.

One of the breakthroughs in DNA testing is the ability to obtain DNA profiles from something as small as a smudged fingerprint, where only very few cells are present.

The Innocence Project

The Innocence Project, an American project, uses DNA profiling to check evidence that has wrongly convicted a person of murder. So far, *The Innocence Project* has pardoned over 200 innocent people.

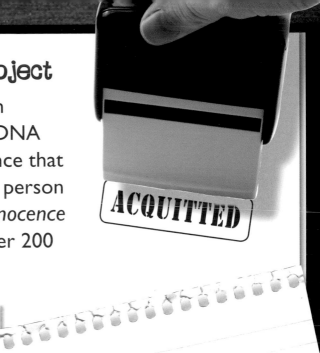

ACQUITTED

A smudged fingerprint may contain DNA.

DIDYOUKNOW?

Red or white?
DNA is always found where white blood cells are present. DNA is found only in a cell's nucleus, and red blood cells do not have nuclei. For example, DNA exists in saliva and hair root follicles.

Evidence in microscopic tummies

Believe it or not, if an insect has fed on a victim, forensic entomologists are able to test the human DNA found in an insect's intestines, possibly matching a corpse to a missing person. Or if an insect has fed on both victim and suspect, the DNA can link those two individuals.

Forensic bugs

Insects on a corpse frequently provide clues that help to determine circumstances surrounding the death. They can help determine the time of death, the location of wounds, whether a body has been moved, and even if drugs were present in the body at the time of death.

Time of death

Forensic entomologists study the life cycle of maggots and flies, together with data on temperature and environmental conditions, to calculate the time of death of a body. Flies rapidly discover a dead body and begin to lay eggs that develop into maggots. Weather conditions will affect the size and development of these eggs or larvae on a corpse.

Maggots

The larva, or maggot, is the main feeding stage of a fly. A maggot can grow from 2–20 mm in four days. It then becomes a pupa, before transforming into a fly.

DIDYOUKNOW?

Big eaters
Maggots can consume 60 per cent of a corpse in less than a week.

UNDERCOVER BUGS

Maggots also reveal secret information contained within the body, such as whether the body contained drugs at the time of death. If a person was under the influence of drugs prior to death, the maggots collect the drugs from the flesh they have eaten. By testing the maggots, scientists can identify the drugs.

Bugs on the move

Bugs on a body may also indicate that a body has been moved, since different surroundings contain different bugs. If someone moved a body after a crime, the insects on the body would not match with the surroundings. Moving a body after bugs have arrived can also mess up the insects' life cycles, alerting forensic entomologists to the move.

The body farm

In the USA, the University of Tennessee Forensic Anthropology Facility has a body farm where scientists study human decomposition after death. It consists of a 3-acre, wooded plot surrounded by a razor wire fence and contains a number of bodies scattered throughout the area. Over 300 people have voluntarily donated their bodies to the body farm. The bodies are exposed in different ways to show how they decompose under various conditions, such as shallow graves, car boots and in the open.

Little carnivores

In one lab test, 48,562 maggots were found on a 156 g piece of meat after 24 hours' exposure. However, because there was insufficient food to sustain them, only 231 flies emerged.

Document analysis

Sometimes, careful study of documents, such as legal documents, can point investigators to a likely suspect or motive.

A document examiner uses various methods to analyse a document, starting with direct visual examination. They may use magnifying lenses, microscopes, and other optical aids including radiation, infrared and ultraviolet lights. The paper and ink of a document can also be chemically analysed.

All document evidence can be broken down into two main categories – handwritten documents, and printed documents.

document inspection under different types of light

Analysing handwritten documents may help to:
- expose forgeries
- confirm a document is genuine
- identify who wrote a document.

Preparing the evidence

Documents that are ready for analysis are placed in thin, clear, plastic folders so the items are protected. They are then marked as exhibits, given a reference number and photographed.

Checking signatures

Firstly, the examiners will compare the signature in question to genuine samples of a person's signature. They will then compare the rhythm and flow of the writing.

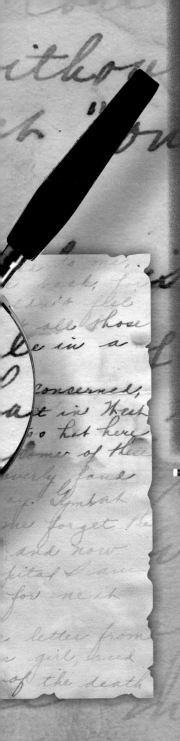

No evidence? What then?

The absence of evidence can sometimes be as helpful as having evidence. This theory is useful when trying to corroborate or disprove the story of victim or suspect.

We can take the example of a shirt that was allegedly cut during a fight involving a knife. After examining the shirt, there was no evidence of cut damage but there was evidence of tear damage. The absence of cut damage helped to disprove the victim's allegation that they had been assaulted with a knife.

Right or left?

Often, a suspect or victim is required to provide samples of their handwriting. Most right-handed people tend to write with a slant to the letters, so that the top of the letters point to the upper right, and the bottom of the letters point to the lower left. The opposite is true for left-handed people. A right-handed person would find it difficult to forge a left-handed person's writing and vice versa.

Dating documents

Forensic scientists can date a document by dating the materials used in the document, such as inks and dyes. This technique is useful but limited. Depending on the ink used, the test can only determine whether a document was produced pre or post 1950!

printing presses

Printed documents

The inkjet printer code

In 2005, scientists discovered that some inkjet and laser printers applied a small series of yellow dots to all pages during the printing process. These yellow dots, when microscopically viewed and decoded, indicated the serial number of the printer, as well as the date and time of the printout. Forensic scientists can trace the serial numbers back to retail sales and individuals, leading to many successes in uncovering illegal printing, such as counterfeiting.

People sometimes try to make counterfeit money.

DIDYOUKNOW?

There are 21 discriminating elements of writing by which one writer is, or may be, distinguished from others. That's a lot of analysis! Different types of handwriting, typewriting, inks and paper can also be analysed. Methods include infrared radiation, ultraviolet radiation, electrostatic detection and microscopy examination.

TOOL MARKINGS AND IMPRESSIONS

Can you spot the cartridge casing?

Tool-mark analysis deals with the impressions or damage made by tools used in a crime.

Firearm analysis, for example, determines if a certain bullet or cartridge came from a particular gun. Empty cartridge casings are the most common items of evidence encountered at the scene of a shooting. Markings that cover a spent cartridge, identify the type of firearm used. If the shooter handled the bullets, fingerprint traces may be present on the cartridge casings. Loading, firing and reloading a weapon can also make impressions on a firearm.

Physical vs. eyewitness

Physical evidence is more reliable than eyewitness testimonies. Experiments have shown that observations made by people witnessing a simulated crime, become increasingly inaccurate over a period of time.

Impression markings

Impression evidence, for example shoe prints or tyre marks, are photographed and sometimes moulds are made so the original item can be identified. Shoe prints can reveal a person's height and weight, while tyre marks may indicate the make and model of a car.

Do any of these match the tracks belonging to the getaway car?

Do any of these match the tool markings we've found?

Forensic footprints

Footprints may reveal not only what type of shoes a suspect wore, but also their likely age, the direction they took, how fast they were going and even if they were carrying anything!

Back at the lab

When the evidence arrives at the lab, a number of teams, including mine, begin to analyse the material. As more tests are completed, facts begin to emerge from our findings.

Back at the lab, our team makes some interesting discoveries!

Fingerprints – Tests on samples reveal there were at least three people who broke into the house, and attacked the victim. Two sets of fingerprints match those found in the police system – both people have prior records for assault and robbery.

The suspects give us their fingerprints.

It's a match!

Tool markings – Markings found on the front door indicate that the intruders forced their way into the victim's house. Tests show that the markings match those made by a crowbar, used to prize open the wooden door.

Document analysis – A number of threatening letters were scattered over the crime scene. Further analysis identifies signature forgeries on a few of them.

Blood and DNA analysis – Blood at the crime scene is a match to the victim's. It is then crosschecked with other splatters found, including those on a vase and on a piece of wood found in the front yard.

This handwriting can be analysed.

Trace evidence – Tests on paint and soil samples, found near shoe prints at the crime scene, indicate that one of the intruders had worn shoes near sand recently. Another pair of shoes had left traces of paint behind. Hair fibres found at the scene are also analysed.

Impressions – A series of shoe prints found on the carpet at the crime scene, are tested and crosschecked.

Myths on TV #1

TV makes evidence analysis appear to be fast and simple, when in reality, crime labs can take weeks or months to analyse and process evidence. Certain chemical processes can take days, and if a piece of evidence has to go through several chemical tests, the process takes even longer.

The suspects' shoes match the prints we found.

What the evidence suggests

From our analysis, police narrow the field of suspects. We conclude from the DNA, fingerprint, and trace-evidence tests, that a group of at least three people participated in the attack and robbery.

After further investigation, police discover that one of the intruders lives right near the beach, accounting for the sand in the shoe prints, while the other was a house painter, explaining the traces of paint left behind.

In the end, with the help of our lab results, police charge four men over the assault and robbery, and recover the stolen money and jewellery.

With our help, the criminals are caught!

Findings concluded and reports are prepared

My team and I compile our findings as police reports, for use in court. On this occasion, I am required to present in court DNA profiling evidence of the four accused men. More often, I am not required to attend a hearing in person. My findings are just submitted to the court as evidence.

A major part of my job is explaining scientific results to non-scientists. We frequently need to clarify our findings to those who have no scientific knowledge, including police officers, lawyers and jury members, so it is crucial that we use minimal scientific jargon when preparing documents.

giving evidence in court

Myths on TV #2

TV crime shows take the job descriptions of approximately five different forensic specialists and combine them into one super scientist – someone who conducts any type of analysis, almost entirely on their own. In reality, a forensics laboratory consists of at least six different sections, where many different forensic specialists analyse one piece of evidence each before deciding if the evidence reveals something.

Follow these steps to become a forensic scientist

1. To be an **Assistant forensic scientist** in England, Wales and Northern Ireland you need at least one A level / two H grades in science subjects and four GCSEs / S grades (A–C/1–3). In Scotland you will need a higher national award in chemistry, biology or the equivalent. In Northern Ireland entry is usually four GCSEs (A–C) although higher-level qualifications are an advantage.

2. **Forensic scientists** will have a good honours degree in maths, science (including forensic science) or an appropriate technology course. These courses will require two A level / three H grades in chemistry, biology and often maths. Other qualifications may be accepted so ask your Connexions / Careers service for more details.

3. **In reality, both forensic scientists and assistants often have postgraduate qualifications and lots of laboratory experience.**

4. To become a **case-reporting forensic scientist** or **forensic science researcher**, you will need at least a good first degree in biology, chemistry or a related subject. In many cases you also need a postgraduate qualification.

5. A driving licence may be an advantage and good colour vision is important.

DIDYOUKNOW?

To work for the Forensic Science Service (FSS) you have to be a British National, a member of the European Union or European Economic Area or a Commonwealth country and have lived in the UK for 3 or more years.

Opportunities for forensic scientists

Most forensic scientists in England and Wales work for **The Forensic Science Service (FSS)** in Birmingham (2 labs), Chepstow, Chorley, Huntingdon, London and Wetherby. It employs over 1,400 forensic scientists and assistants. Occasionally they offer trainee posts.

In Scotland they work mainly for **the police**, with labs in Glasgow, Edinburgh, Aberdeen and Dundee. They employ about 175 people.

In Northern Ireland, they are part of the **Civil Service** and employ about 100 people in these jobs. There are a few private companies and also organisations which focus on specific areas of forensic science such as fire investigation, questioned documents, and advising the Armed Forces and the Ministry of Defence.

investigating possible arson

You could work at a private lab.

OTHER RELATED CAREER AREAS TO CONSIDER:

- Scenes of Crime Officer (SOCOs)
- Biochemist
- Hospital laboratory worker
- Biologist
- Chemist
- Pharmacist
- Clinical Scientist
- Microbiologist
- Pharmacologist
- Toxicologist

DIDYOUKNOW?

What will I earn?
Trainees usually earn £13,000–£17,000 a year depending on their qualifications. With 2 or 3 years experience it could be £19,000–over £30,000. Heads of departments can earn £50,000+.

Useful contacts

Connexions / Careers Service and UCAS www.ucas.ac.uk

For details of university degree courses, ask your Connexions / Careers Service or look at the UCAS website.

The Forensic Science Society www.forensic-science-society.org.uk

18a Mount Parade, Harrogate HG1 1BX Tel: 01423 506 068

The Forensic Science Service (FSS) www.forensic.gov.uk

Trident Court, 2920 Solihull Parkway, Birmingham Business Park, Birmingham B37 7YN
Tel: 01213 295 200

Forensic Science Northern Ireland (FSNI) www.fsni.gov.uk

151 Belfast Road, Carrickfergus, County Antrim, Ireland BT38 8PL Tel: 02090 361 888
For careers information contact: forensic.science@fsni.gov.uk

Grampian Police Force Science Laboratory www.grampianpolicecareers.co.uk

Queen Street, Aberdeen AB10 1ZA Tel: 0845 600 7500

Lothian and Borders Police Forensic Science Laboratory

www.lbp.police.uk/forensicscience

11 Howdenhall Road, Edinburgh EH16 6TF Tel: 0131 666 1212

Police Forensic Science Laboratory Dundee www.pfsld.com

West Bell Street, Dundee DD1 9JU Tel: 01382 596 577

Strathclyde Police Force Support Department www.strathclyde.police.uk

173 Pitt Street, Glasgow G2 4JS Tel: 0141 532 2000

Further information

Explore Forensics www.exploreforensics.co.uk

This is a great reference point for information on forensic science and crime scene investigations. Learn more about the different types of forensic science and the use of forensics in crime scene investigation and pathology.

The New Scientist www.newscientist.com

This weekly magazine features all types of articles on scientific issues, and also includes a job listing.

Skills for Justice www.skillsforjustice.com

9 Riverside Court, Don Road, Sheffield S9 2TJ Tel: 0114 261 1499

Skills for Justice is the Sector Skills Council and Standards Setting Body for the Justice sector.

Glossary

arson – to deliberately set fire to something

assault – a violent attack on someone

botanical – referring to the scientific study of plants

cartridge – a tube containing a bullet and an explosive substance; used in guns

collecting official – crime scene investigator who collects and bags evidence

corroborate – to confirm that something is true

counterfeit – something made to look genuine, in order to deceive people

deduce – to work something out from other facts

entombed – to put something in a place that is hidden or very deep

fallible – likely to be wrong or misleading

follicles – small sacs or cavities in the body, e.g. hair follicles

fraud – something that deceives people in an illegal or immoral way

gestation – the time during which a foetus is growing inside its mother's womb

homicide – the crime of murder

infallible – incapable of making a mistake

jargon – words that are used in special or technical ways by particular groups of people

microscopy – an investigation, observation, or experiment that involves the use of a microscope

nucleus – the central part of an atom or cell

pathologist – a doctor or scientist who studies the nature and cause of disease

perpetrators – people who do, or are responsible for, something; usually criminal

rectified – corrected

sickle – a short-handled tool with a curved blade; used for cutting tall grass or grain

simulated – something that is copied; made a pretence of

specialists – people who have a particular skill or who know a lot about a particular subject

tamper – to interfere with or damage something

vaults – strong, secure rooms where valuables are stored; burial chambers

Index

other titles in the series

PILOT

EMERGENCY **NURSE**

TV PRODUCER

MAGAZINE **EDITOR**

GAME DEVELOPER

MOTOR MECHANIC

ANIMATOR

BUILDER

CHEF

SPORTS TRAINER

FASHION DESIGNER